Read for a Better World™

CONCRETE MIXERS

A First Look

ZELDA WAGNER

Lerner Publications ◆ Minneapolis

Educator Toolbox

Reading books is a great way for kids to express what they're interested in. Before reading this title, ask the reader these questions:

What do you think this book is about? Look at the cover for clues.

What do you already know about concrete mixers?

What do you want to learn about concrete mixers?

Let's Read Together

Encourage the reader to use the pictures to understand the text.

Point out when the reader successfully sounds out a word.

Praise the reader for recognizing sight words such as *go* and *the*.

TABLE OF CONTENTS

Concrete Mixers

Concrete mixers mix, carry, and pour concrete.

Concrete mixers bring concrete to places. Concrete makes buildings strong.

Where might concrete mixers bring concrete?

The driver sits in the cab. A water tank and a drum are behind the cab.

The drum makes concrete.

Sand, cement, and small rocks go in first.

Water from the tank goes in next. Then the drum spins.

The truck drives.
The drum spins and
mixes concrete.

Wet concrete pours down the chute.

A worker makes the concrete smooth.

What tools could the worker use to make the concrete smooth?

The concrete dries. It is hard. It makes sidewalks and bridges.

What else could concrete make?

Concrete mixers stir and spin.
They make concrete to build things!

You Connect!

Have you ever seen a concrete mixer?

Would you want to drive a concrete mixer?

How can you learn more about concrete mixers?

STEM Snapshot

Encourage students to think and ask questions like scientists. Ask the reader:

What is something you learned about concrete mixers?

What is something you noticed about concrete mixer parts?

What is something you still want to learn about concrete mixers?

Photo Glossary

Learn More

Bolte, Mari. *Concrete Mixers*. Mankato, MN: Creative Education and Creative Paperbacks, 2024.

Eick, Jean. *Concrete Mixers*. Parker, CO: Child's World, 2023.

Wagner, Zelda. *Dump Trucks: A First Look*. Minneapolis: Lerner Publications, 2025.

Index

Photo Acknowledgments

Image credits: BanksPhotos/Getty Images, p. 5; aire images/Getty Images, p. 6; poco_bw/Getty Images, p. 7; szmarinov/Getty Images, p. 8; JETSADAPHOTO/Getty Images, p. 10; Sergio Mendoza Hochmann/Getty Images, p. 11; alvarez/Getty Images, p. 13; FGorgun/Getty Images, p. 14; Alistair Berg/Getty Images, p. 16; Thanit Weerawan/Getty Images, p. 17; aaaaimages/Getty Images, p. 18; xia yuan/Getty Images, p. 19; Iryna Melnyk/Getty Images, p. 20.
Cover: Andyqwe/Getty Images.

Lerner Publications Company
An imprint of Lerner Publishing Group, Inc.
241 First Avenue North
Minneapolis, MN 55401 USA

For reading levels and more information, look up this title at www.lernerbooks.com.

Main body text set in Mikado Medium.
Typeface provided by Hannes von Doehren.

Library of Congress Cataloging-in-Publication Data

Names: Wagner, Zelda, 2000- author.
Title: Concrete mixers : a first look / Zelda Wagner.
Description: Minneapolis : Lerner Publications, [2025] | Series: Read about construction vehicles | Includes bibliographical references and index. | Audience: Ages 5–8 | Audience: Grades K–1 | Summary: "Concrete mixers stir and pour concrete. And they drive it from place to place! Readers explore the different parts of these construction vehicles"—Provided by publisher.
Identifiers: LCCN 2024007753 (print) | LCCN 2024007754 (ebook) | ISBN 9798765647820 (lib. bdg.) | ISBN 9798765657195 (epub)
Subjects: LCSH: Concrete mixers—Juvenile literature.
Classification: LCC TA439 .W337 2025 (print) | LCC TA439 (ebook) | DDC 624.1/8340284—dc23/eng/20240314

LC record available at https://lccn.loc.gov/2024007753
LC ebook record available at https://lccn.loc.gov/2024007754

ISBN 979-8-7656-6220-5 (pbk.)

Manufactured in the United States of America
1-1010888-53343-5/17/2024